CONTENTS

INTRODUCTION

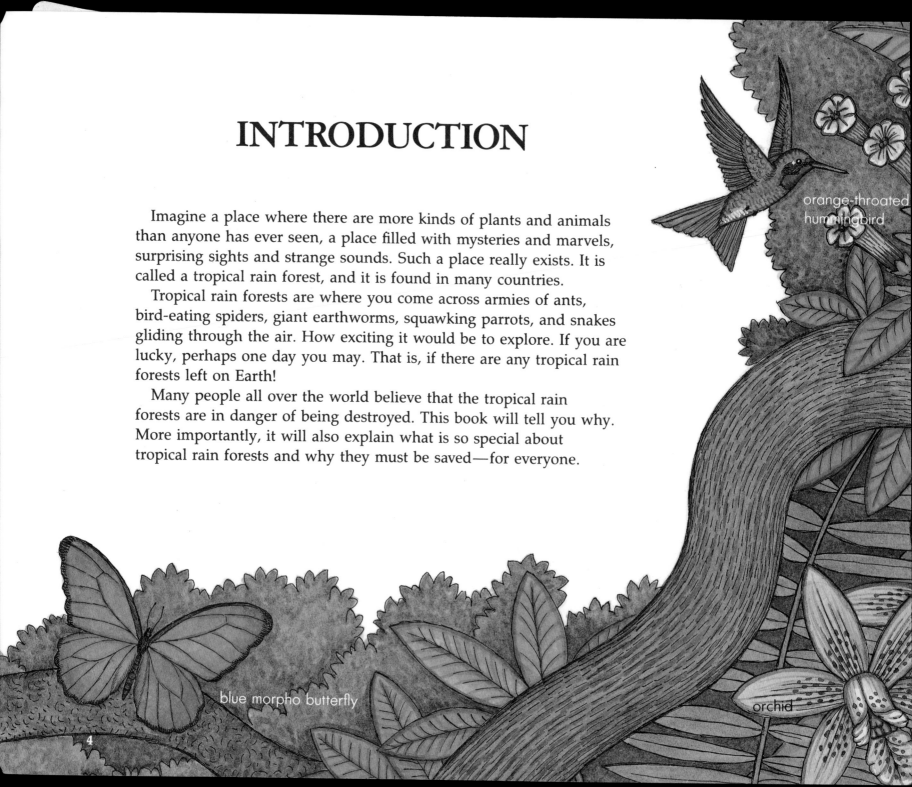

Imagine a place where there are more kinds of plants and animals than anyone has ever seen, a place filled with mysteries and marvels, surprising sights and strange sounds. Such a place really exists. It is called a tropical rain forest, and it is found in many countries.

Tropical rain forests are where you come across armies of ants, bird-eating spiders, giant earthworms, squawking parrots, and snakes gliding through the air. How exciting it would be to explore. If you are lucky, perhaps one day you may. That is, if there are any tropical rain forests left on Earth!

Many people all over the world believe that the tropical rain forests are in danger of being destroyed. This book will tell you why. More importantly, it will also explain what is so special about tropical rain forests and why they must be saved—for everyone.

orange-throated hummingbird

blue morpho butterfly

orchid

Why Save the Rain Forest?

HAYNER PUBLIC LIBRARY DISTRICT-ALTON

0 00 30 01906282

Written by Donald Silver   **Illustrated by Patricia J. Wynne**

Julian ⓂⓂ Messner

HAYNER PUBLIC LIBRARY DISTRICT
ALTON, ILLINOIS
BRANCH

Copyright © 1993 by Donald Silver
Illustrations © 1993 by Patricia Wynne

All rights reserved including the right of
reproduction in whole or in part in any form.
Published by Julian Messner, a division of
Simon & Schuster, Simon & Schuster Building,
Rockefeller Center, 1230 Avenue of the
Americas, New York, NY 10020.

JULIAN MESSNER and colophon are trademarks of
Simon & Schuster.

Manufactured in the United States of America

10 9 8 7 6 5 4 3 2 1 (LSB)
10 9 8 7 6 5 4 3 2 1 (pbk.)

Library of Congress Cataloging-in-Publication Data

Silver, Donald M., 1947–
   Why save the rain forest? / by Donald Silver : illustrated by
Patricia Wynne.
      p.   cm.
   Includes bibliographical references and index.
   Summary: Explains what a rain forest is and where they
are found, the dangers they face, and the importance of
protecting their plant and animal life.
   1. Rain forest--Juvenile literature. 2. Rain forest
conservation--Juvenile literature. 3. Rain forest
fauna--Juvenile literature. 4. Rain forest plants--Juvenile
literature. [1. Rain forest. 2. Rain forest ecology.
3. Ecology.] I. Wynne, Patricia, ill. II. Title.
QH86.S55 1993
33.75′16′0913—dc20   93-22313
                                            CIP
                                            AC
ISBN 0-671-86609-5(LSB)   ISBN 0-671-86610- 9(pbk.)

For
Marguerite Grey
who loves all the plants
and animals

Rain forests are full of living things, large and small.

golden lion marmoset

liana vine

tree lizard

palm

5

1 IN A TROPICAL RAIN FOREST

The evening downpour has stopped, and the air is hot and damp. Coiled in the dead leaves on the forest floor waits the most dangerous snake in Central America, the *fer-de-lance*. To satisfy its hunger, the snake pierces its venom-filled fangs into a scurrying mouse. Within seconds the venom goes to work. Nerves are paralyzed, and cells are destroyed.

The *fer-de-lance* will not be enjoying another meal. From out of nowhere, a large *mussurana* snake attacks. The frightened *fer-de-lance* bites, releasing every drop of venom into the attacker. Nothing happens, and the *mussurana* makes a snack of the *fer-de-lance*. Something inside the *mussurana* has caused the deadly poison of the *fer-de-lance* to become harmless. What could it be?

Thousands of miles away, in Central Africa, the juicy miracle fruit grows. It tastes so sweet that after chewing one of its berries you could bite into a lemon without noticing its sour nip. The sweetness of the miracle fruit doesn't come from sugar, however. It comes from a protein that is thousands of times sweeter. What is this protein, and how does it work?

mussurana

fer-de-lance

Rafflesia flower

Around the globe, in Southeast Asia, what looks like a big red cabbage on the bare ground slowly starts to open. Over four days, leathery petals unfurl into *Rafflesia*, the largest flower in the world. This huge flower spans three feet across and weighs 36 pounds. Don't go too close though. *Rafflesia* smells like a gigantic, rotting hamburger. How does a flower grow so large, and what makes it smell like meat? The answers to all of these questions can be found in the tropical rain forests.

The Hot Band Around the Equator

Tropical rain forests grow in the hot band around the equator called the tropics. These lush forests cover the land like a vast, green carpet. Every day of the year the sun shines on the forests for about 12 hours. Every day of the year there are about 12 hours of darkness. Every day the forest temperature hovers around 80°F—even in winter. It is always hot, humid, and rainy in these forests. It rains a *lot*. In one year, 100 to 400 inches of water fall on the trees. That's up to twenty times as much rain as falls on New York City or San Francisco.

Rain forests can also be found in places where the climate is more moderate. The rain forest in the northwestern part of the United States is green, moist, and cool. This book focuses on tropical rain forests.

uakari monkey

click b

tree a

blue morpho butterfly

iridescent beetle

common iguana

pygmy marmoset

8

A Very Different World

Walk in a forest near where you live and you may see a dozen or so kinds of trees that reach 50 to 90 feet tall. There will be squirrels running along branches, birds hunting for food, bees and other insects buzzing by, and perhaps butterflies searching for flowers.

Stroll the same distance through a tropical rain forest and you'll pass by hundreds of kinds of trees. Many tower more than 125 feet with tangles of thick vines hanging down. Orchids, ferns, and other exotic plants grow directly on their branches. You'll see few, if any, animals because they are well hidden in the dense leaves. But all around you there are hundreds of kinds of birds, frogs, and mammals, and tens of thousands of kinds of insects in a rainbow of colors and with more patterns than you can imagine. No place on Earth is more filled with life. Since no life has yet been discovered on any other planet, tropical rain forests may well be the most alive places in the universe.

hoatzin

jaguar

caiman lizard

Hercules beetle

9

2 SHRINKING FAST

When you ride through a city or town, try to imagine it as a forest. At one time, it may have been. Men and women cleared the land to make room for homes, farms, roads, and schools. By doing so, they hoped to build a better life for themselves and their children.

While millions of trees were cut down in Europe and the United States, the tropical rain forests were hardly touched by settlers. Yet the vast tropical carpet of green covered twice as much land as it does today. What caused the rain forests to shrink?

Some Reasons Why

Over the past 100 years, the number of people living on Earth has grown larger and larger. Every year there has been more and more demand for food, houses, clothing, furniture, medicine, electricity, and fuels. Many nations north of the tropics became wealthy by growing food and building factories to meet the demands of the increasing world population. In the tropics, though, most people remained poor and landless. They had little or no chance of improving their way of life. So they turned to their forest land as the Europeans and Americans had done before them.

Slowly at first, then at a faster and faster pace, they began to cut down their forests. Technology helped speed their work. Armed with chain saws, people could slice through a hundred-year-old tree in minutes. Before long, farms, cattle ranches, logging camps, mines, and oil drills replaced beetles, bats, birds, and butterflies feeding, nesting, flying, and hiding.

Every second of every day a piece of rain forest the size of a football field disappears. If nothing is done to stop this process, all of the rain forests will be gone within your lifetime. That's why in newspapers and magazines, on television and in films, in books and on T-shirts, people all over the world are calling for the destruction to end.

But why should the people in the tropics listen? Shouldn't they be able to use their land any way they want? Shouldn't they be able to build better lives and help their countries to prosper?

Only by understanding how important the rain forests are can *all* people decide.

11

3 A PART OF YOUR LIFE

When you sit down to dinner, shop at the mall, water the house plants, or fly in a plane, the rain forests may be touching your life.

Look at the foods you eat, for instance. Corn, rice, and tomatoes were first discovered growing in a tropical rain forest. Sprinkle cinnamon on toast. Mix vanilla in cake frosting. These and many other spices that add flavor to your food come from tropical rain forests. So do tea, coffee, cocoa, sugar, pineapples, bananas, Brazil nuts, and chocolate.

One of the best known rain-forest plants is the rubber tree. Its milky sap called latex is made into strong natural rubber that resists heat. If you have ever flown in an airplane, you landed safely on tires made of natural rubber.

Chemicals in rain-forest leaves, flowers, and seeds are used to make cosmetics and perfumes, polishes and soaps, cough drops and chewing gum. Tough fibers in ropes and cords, cane furniture, woven baskets, and many shade-loving indoor plants all come from the tropical rain forests.

rubber plant

latex

Without knowing it, hundreds of millions of people take medicines containing chemicals that come from rain-forest plants. These chemicals can kill germs, reduce fever, lower blood pressure, relax muscles, and make rashes disappear.

A Very Special Plant

Thanks to the rain forests, there is a very strong medicine that overcomes one kind of leukemia—cancer of white blood cells—in children. This kind of leukemia once killed most children suffering from it. But today, with chemicals made by the rosy periwinkle plant, nearly all such children can be saved.

More than 2,000 rain-forest plants have been discovered containing chemicals that doctors can give to treat deadly cancers in adults. In no other part of the world do so many cancer-fighting plants grow.

It is possible to produce thousands of products made from parts of rain-forest plants without destroying the forests themselves. More leaves, flowers, fruits, seeds, and sap will keep forming as long as the rain forests stand.

rosy periwinkle

4 A HOME TO MANY LIVING THINGS

Men and women have gathered a wealth of information about Earth, the solar system, and the universe. Yet no one knows how many kinds of living things there are on this planet, mostly because people haven't been able to fully explore the rain forests. Come along on an imaginary walk through one and you will soon know why.

A Walk Along the Forest Floor

There is some type of life just about everywhere in a tropical rain forest. The soil teems with bacteria and other creatures too small to be seen without a microscope. Underground funguses help tree roots absorb minerals without disturbing the worms, insects, and snails around them. Shoots of new plants push up from the forest floor.

To snakes the forest floor is the place to wait for prey. To cockroaches, slugs, and centipedes it offers stones, leaves, and logs to hide under. To army ants, it is a highway for millions of soldiers to mount an attack on lizards, scorpions, and small mammals. And to armadillos and wild pigs, it is the perfect spot to dig for insects or roots.

It's easy to walk along the rain forest floor. There are few flowering plants or shrubs to get in your way. Only plants that like shade are able to grow here. The sun may be brightly shining but little light reaches the ground—it is almost all blocked out by a canopy of leaves 100 feet or more above you.

carpenter ants

fer-de-lance

iridescent beetle

spiny mouse

moss

agouti

climbing vine

antbird

army ants

88 butterfly

centipede

gold frog

Where Short Trees Grow

   As you walk along you'll notice that not all rain-forest trees reach great heights. There are shorter trees and plants that make up the layer of the rain forest called the understory. Like the rest of the lower rain forest, the understory is shady, making it hard to locate insects that look like sticks, spiders weaving webs, or a jaguar snoozing on a branch. If you take your time and look closely, however, you will be able to spot termite nests the size of soccer balls, flowers blooming directly out of tree trunks, and the bright colors of poisonous frogs warning you and all animals to stay away.

climbing vine

green vine snake

jaguar

green-headed tanager

poison dart frog

stick insect

Up in the Canopy

Follow the trunks of the trees as they rise straight up from the forest floor. You'll see them open like umbrellas, branching out to form the rooflike canopy of the rain forest. In this dense layer of green, leaves bathed in full sunlight absorb energy and use it to make food.

Imagine sitting high up in the canopy. Beautiful orchids, cactuses, ferns, and pineapple-like plants grow on tree branches. These epiphytes, or air plants, don't need soil to grow. All around you vines dangle down to the understory. These vines often tie leafy branches of one tree to those of its neighbors.

More animals live in the canopy than in any other forest layer. Among the leaves there are screeching parrots, playful monkeys, leaping lizards, sleeping bats, berry-eating toucans, hovering hummingbirds, and fantastic beetles. Many of these animals spend their entire lives in the canopy moving from branch to branch. Since they don't come down, there is no way of knowing how many kinds of animals exist without climbing into the canopy to find out.

kapok tree

harpy eagle

people exploring the canopy

capuchin monkey

18

Over the Top

Towering above the canopy are the tops of the tallest trees. Hidden in these rain-forest giants are eagles, hawks, and other birds of prey peering down for monkeys, sloths, and snakes to seize in their powerful claws. If you were a passenger in a low-flying airplane, you might catch a glimpse of a harpy eagle diving down into the canopy, but the brilliant shiny blue of Morpho butterflies would more likely catch your eye.

Calling for Explorers

Creatures live at every level of the rain forest—on, inside, and under tree bark, inside hollow trees and dead logs, on top of and under leaves, inside fruits, in water trapped in cup-shaped plants, on animal skin and beneath it.

Fully exploring just one rain forest to discover all of the creatures living there means poking around in every possible spot. Explorers must figure out how to move about and work in the treetops. They must also find ways of protecting themselves from the heat, humidity, drenching rains, and biting insects.

Suppose you became a rain-forest explorer. What discoveries might await you? Many scientists now think that there are millions of species, or kinds, of living things waiting to be discovered in rain forests around the world. It is possible that up to 90 percent of all species living on Earth come from tropical rain forests.

Rain-forest species cannot be moved somewhere else. They aren't able to survive where winters are cold. They have to stay right where they are. The destruction of the rain forests means the end of a home for rain-forest species. By saving the rain forests, people will help countless numbers of species to live.

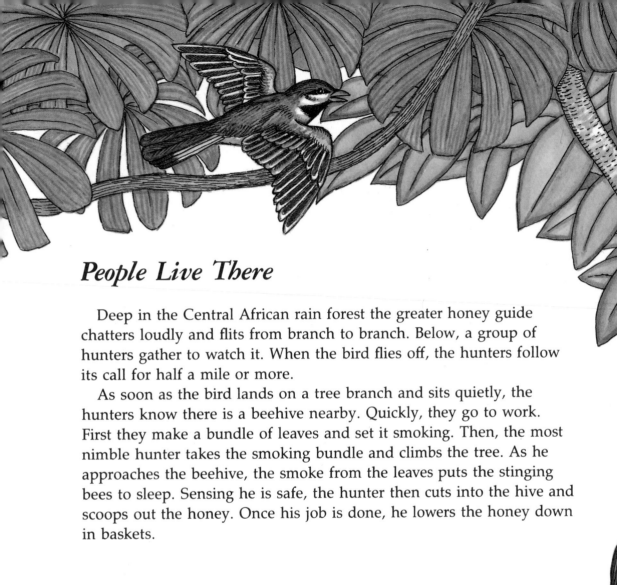

People Live There

Deep in the Central African rain forest the greater honey guide chatters loudly and flits from branch to branch. Below, a group of hunters gather to watch it. When the bird flies off, the hunters follow its call for half a mile or more.

As soon as the bird lands on a tree branch and sits quietly, the hunters know there is a beehive nearby. Quickly, they go to work. First they make a bundle of leaves and set it smoking. Then, the most nimble hunter takes the smoking bundle and climbs the tree. As he approaches the beehive, the smoke from the leaves puts the stinging bees to sleep. Sensing he is safe, the hunter then cuts into the hive and scoops out the honey. Once his job is done, he lowers the honey down in baskets.

Perfect Partners

When the hunters leave, the honey guide flies over to the open hive to feast on the beeswax left behind. None of the hunters would think of killing a honey guide. The hunters need these birds to locate

precious honey for them. The birds also need the hunters. On its own, the honey guide would be unable to open the hive with its short beak.

The people of the Central African rain forest spend their entire lives gathering fruits and berries, trapping wild hogs in nets, and capturing parrots and monkeys with poisoned arrows. They have no refrigerators, cars, computers, televisions, or supermarkets. They must find everything they need to survive in the rain forest.

For tens of thousands of years people have lived in the rain forest and have learned its secrets. They know which plants and animals to eat, which to avoid, and which ones can be used to make medicines. They use branches to build shelters, and to make tools and weapons. For generations they have passed this information and more along to their children and grandchildren. Most importantly, they do all this without destroying the rain forest. They cannot understand why any human being would want to permanently harm the rain forest.

Don't the people of the rain forest have a right to keep living where they want especially since they know more about their home than anyone else?

The honey guide waits as the hunter climbs to the beehive.

greater honey guide

21

A Source of New Foods and Medicines

What would you say if you walked into the school lunchroom and found the following on the menu?:

WINGED BEAN SOUP
MANIOC STEW
PATAUÁ and TACUMA DELIGHT

You might wonder what the school was trying to feed you.

As it turns out, winged bean is a vegetable that is high in protein. Manioc is a plant root rich in starch that is also used to make tapioca. Both patauá and tacuma are palm fruits full of vitamins and protein. People in many countries eat these rain-forest foods all the time.

Although you may never have eaten patauá or tacuma, your children might find them on their school lunch plates. As the number of people living on Earth continues to grow, there will be more and more demand for food. Perhaps, if the rain forests aren't destroyed, there will be time to learn from the people still living there about the many kinds of foods they eat. Explorers, too, will be able to search the forests for yet undiscovered plants and animals safe for humans to eat.

green pineapple

Amazonian yam

cashew nuts

winged beans

manioc root

22

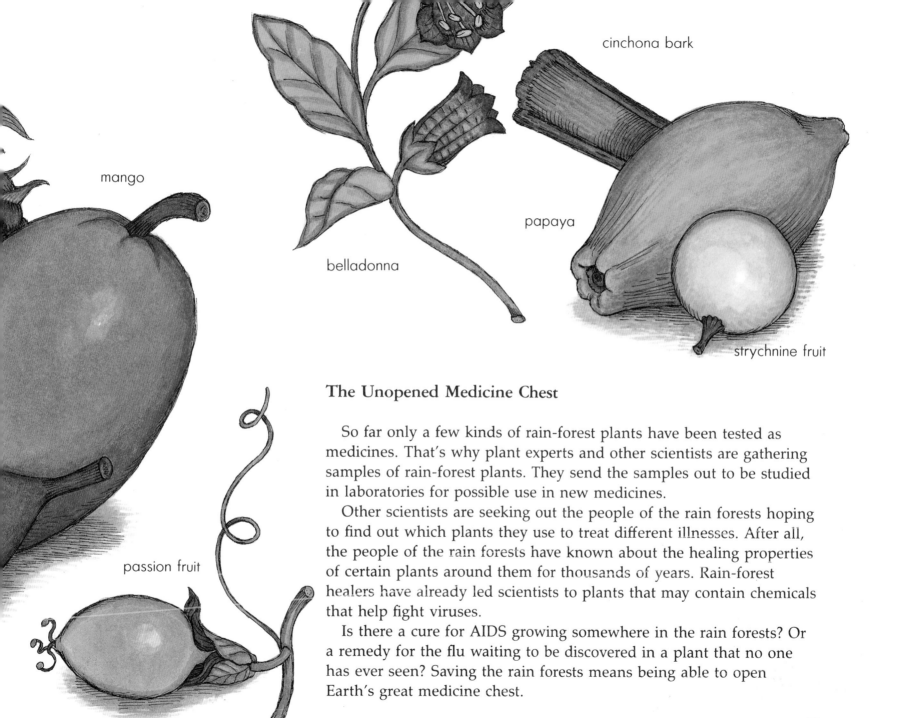

mango

cinchona bark

belladonna

papaya

strychnine fruit

passion fruit

The Unopened Medicine Chest

So far only a few kinds of rain-forest plants have been tested as medicines. That's why plant experts and other scientists are gathering samples of rain-forest plants. They send the samples out to be studied in laboratories for possible use in new medicines.

Other scientists are seeking out the people of the rain forests hoping to find out which plants they use to treat different illnesses. After all, the people of the rain forests have known about the healing properties of certain plants around them for thousands of years. Rain-forest healers have already led scientists to plants that may contain chemicals that help fight viruses.

Is there a cure for AIDS growing somewhere in the rain forests? Or a remedy for the flu waiting to be discovered in a plant that no one has ever seen? Saving the rain forests means being able to open Earth's great medicine chest.

Nature's Secrets of Survival Are There

In the canopy of a South American rain forest, a butterfly and a plant are at war. The plant, the passionflower vine, adds splashes of color to the surrounding greens with its spiky flowers. Millions of insects would love to turn the vine's leaves into their favorite restaurant, but don't dare to take a bite. The reason? The leaves are filled with insect-killing poison.

Watch closely, though. Fluttering in and out of the passionflowers are long-winged butterflies streaked with brilliant bands of yellow, orange, or red. These are Heliconid butterflies and they use their long mouth tubes to sip sweet flower nectar. When it is time for the butterflies to lay their yellow eggs, the passionflower leaves provide the perfect spot.

Once the eggs hatch, the emerging caterpillars chomp into the vine's leaves without being harmed by the poison. Why? The caterpillars are able to store the poison inside their bodies. They use it as a weapon against birds that eat caterpillars. The bright colors of the caterpillars serve as a warning to the birds. If a bird ignores the warning and eats one, it will spit out the caterpillar. The bird learns quickly what it can and cannot eat.

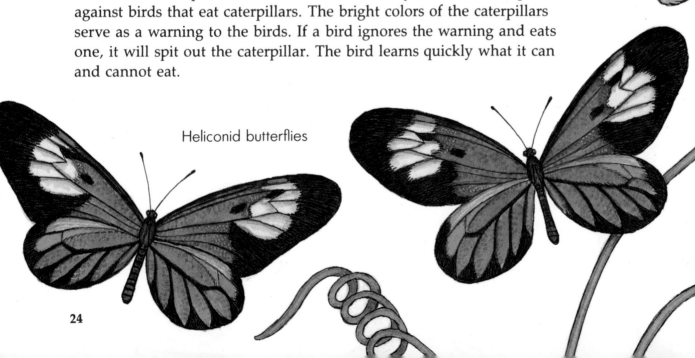

Heliconid butterflies

24

chrysalis

egg

passionflower

Heliconid caterpillar

In about three weeks, the caterpillars reach full size and change into butterflies. During this change the vine's poison doesn't disappear but is now stored in the butterflies' bodies. The birds of the rain forest soon realize that the butterflies' colors also spell POISON! They avoid the butterflies, too.

To save its leaves from the Heliconid caterpillars, the passionflower vine tries to trick the butterflies. How? It grows leaves that look like the leaves on nearby trees. If a Heliconid butterfly overlooks the vine and lays eggs on the nearby trees, that's one passionflower vine saved from the caterpillars. The passionflower vine has other tricks. It grows leaves with yellow spots that match the shape and color of the butterfly eggs. Since a Heliconid butterfly won't lay eggs on a leaf that already has eggs, the butterfly will keep searching for an unoccupied leaf.

Some passionflower vines do battle by growing leaves with tiny hooked hairs that stab and kill caterpillars. Others call in troops of ants for help. Those passionflower vines make a sweet liquid that the ants can't resist. In return, the ants attack the Heliconid caterpillars to keep them from harming the vine that feeds them.

All Connected

The war between the passionflower vine and the Heliconid butterfly has been going on for millions of years. Whatever methods the vine had of getting rid of the Heliconids, the butterflies had ways of staying around. The survival of the butterflies, ants, and passionflower vines became tightly linked together. So, too, are the lives of many other rain-forest species.

Just as people who work in stores, factories, hospitals, and offices depend upon each other to meet the needs of your city or town, the plants and animals of the rain forests depend on each other, too. They cannot survive on their own. Now try to imagine your town without police, firefighters, grocers, or garbage collectors. It would cease to be a place where most people could live. The same is true for the rain forests. Each piece of rain forest that is cut down removes workers vital to the life of the forest. No one knows how many species a rain forest can lose before the forest itself dies.

Staying Alive

The rain forests are special because of the many unusual ways their species have of surviving. Nature uses colors, shapes, patterns, disguises, sticky tongues, curling tails, stinging hairs—whatever it takes—to give each species the best chance of staying alive. To stay alive, some plants wind up helping animals and some animals help plants. The passionflower vine makes poison to stay alive. So does the *fer-de-lance* snake. The largest flower in the world, *Rafflesia*, smells like rotten hamburger to attract flies that feed on dead animals. When the fooled flies land on the flower, pollen sticks to their bodies and is carried to other *Rafflesias* nearby where the flies are fooled again. Without this pollen transfer, the *Rafflesia* cannot reproduce.

deadleaf butterfly

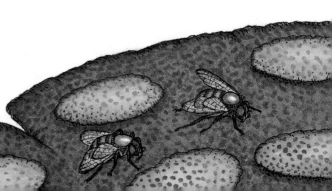

The Rafflesia flower smells like rotten meat and attracts flies.

The hooded Pitohui is the only bird known to have poisonous feathers.

People use the miracle plant from Costa Rica to make medicines.

The rain forests don't produce a fruit, flower, or poison just so people can be happier or healthier. Because humans eat fruits like other animals, and fight the same kinds of germs that attack plants and animals, they have learned how to use nature's secrets of survival to improve their lives and to fight disease. The more rain-forest secrets that are unlocked, the more people can take advantage of nature's way of getting jobs done and keeping living things disease-free. The secrets will be around as long as the rain forests are.

5 WHY SAVE THE RAIN FORESTS?

To Protect the Plants That Feed You

In spring, go for a walk in the park or woods. If you see a flash of yellow or red, it might be a yellow warbler or a scarlet tanager visiting for a day or two. Like millions of other tropical rain-forest birds, these visitors are on their way north to spend the summer. In autumn, the birds may again stop over in your park or woods on their way back to the rain forest. These rain-forest visitors delight birdwatchers and help farmers get rid of insects that destroy crops.

Farmers need all the help they can get to keep insects from ruining their crops. For decades, farmers have sprayed chemicals called pesticides to kill bugs and other pests. There are serious drawbacks to the use of pesticides, however. They harm people, pollute water, and poison the soil. Today many insect pests are no longer killed by the chemicals. The crops people depend on for food have also changed. They don't resist diseases as strongly as they once did.

yellow warbler

28

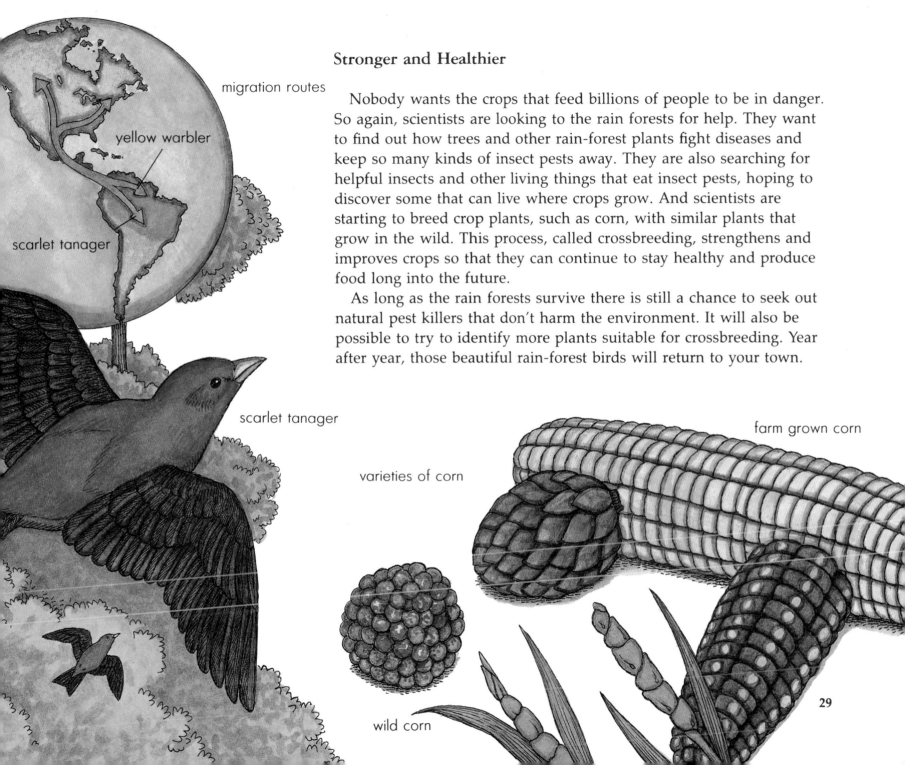

Stronger and Healthier

Nobody wants the crops that feed billions of people to be in danger. So again, scientists are looking to the rain forests for help. They want to find out how trees and other rain-forest plants fight diseases and keep so many kinds of insect pests away. They are also searching for helpful insects and other living things that eat insect pests, hoping to discover some that can live where crops grow. And scientists are starting to breed crop plants, such as corn, with similar plants that grow in the wild. This process, called crossbreeding, strengthens and improves crops so that they can continue to stay healthy and produce food long into the future.

As long as the rain forests survive there is still a chance to seek out natural pest killers that don't harm the environment. It will also be possible to try to identify more plants suitable for crossbreeding. Year after year, those beautiful rain-forest birds will return to your town.

migration routes

yellow warbler

scarlet tanager

scarlet tanager

varieties of corn

farm grown corn

wild corn

29

To Keep the Water Cycling

It can begin with a few drops. Or the darkened sky can burst open with thick sheets of water. Just when it seems that it has rained all it could, there is another downpour that doesn't stop for days. So much wetness is exactly what a rain forest needs to stay alive. But what happens to all the water?

Go outside after a rainstorm and feel how wet the soil is. Water that didn't soak into the ground runs off into streams and rivers or into reservoirs that hold water for people to use. The same is true in the rain forest, except in the rain forest there is a lot more rain a lot more often than where you live.

Almost half of all the rain that falls on all the countries of the world falls on rain forests. That's trillions and trillions of gallons. Why doesn't all that rain cause terrible floods? The answer lies beneath the floor of the rain forest. There, the roots of rain-forest plants help trap water in the soil. These roots then slowly release the water into rivers and streams. Eventually, the water is carried hundreds of miles away to farms and to people in towns and cities. They use it for drinking and irrigating their crops.

Inside Plants and Out Again

The roots also absorb water into plants. That water rises up the stem to the leaves. All plant parts need water to work properly, but leaves also use water to make food. Rarely does a plant need all of the water it absorbs from the soil. From tiny openings, leaves release the unused water into the air as a gas called water vapor.

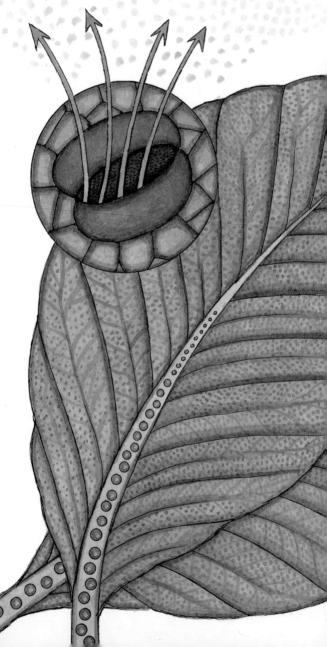

Water vapor escapes through tiny holes in leaves.

Water rises from the roots to the leaves.

water vapor

rain

The illustration shows how water vapor forms clouds and *more* rain. This process takes place everywhere, but because there are so many plants in a rain forest giving off water vapor, a lot of the rain that falls on a rain forest comes from the forest itself. It is recycled over and over again.

If too much rain forest is cut down, there will be less water recycled and less and less rain. Without enough rain, the forest that remains will start to dry out. New plants won't be able to grow. Flooding will increase as plant roots disappear and the fresh water supply to people living in cities and towns will be in danger. Letting the rain forests keep recycling water makes a lot more sense.

Just Dig into the Soil

As you read this, farmers are slashing vines and cutting down trees in a rain forest somewhere on Earth. Cattle ranchers are doing the same. Instead of removing the slashed and cut plants, they burn them. Then, before planting their crops, they mix the ashes into the soil. The farmers and ranchers seem to know what they are doing, but do they?

Dig into soil where you live and most likely you will find a dark top layer that reaches more than a foot deep. This layer is the topsoil. It is rich in minerals and other nutrients plants need to grow and stay healthy.

If you could dig into most rain-forest soils, you would discover only an inch or two of topsoil. It contains few minerals or other nutrients. That is why the farmers and ranchers must mix the ashes into it. The ashes have minerals and nutrients that were stored in the plants before they were burned. Without the ashes, planted crops and grasses could not grow in the rain-forest soil.

The problem is that the mixed-in nutrients do not last. Crops remove some from the soil in order to grow. Rain washes away most of the rest. With the trees gone, the soil bakes in the hot sun. After a few years, crops fail and the farmers and ranchers have to move deeper into the forest. They start their cycle of cutting, slashing, and burning plants once again. Over and over the destruction continues, yet the soil never improves. Even if an entire rain forest is cut and burned, no one will be able to grow crops on the land. The one thing that can grow on such soil is a rain forest.

Will the farmers and ranchers learn that what they are doing won't work in time for the rest of the world to study the rain forests and figure out how nature *does* make things work?

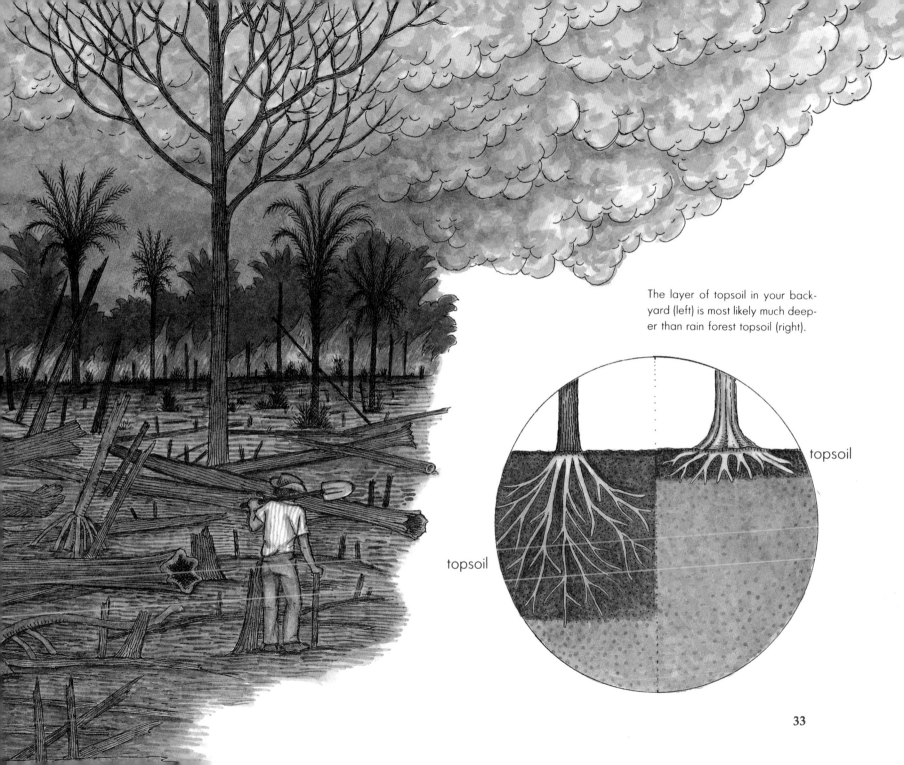

The layer of topsoil in your back-
yard (left) is most likely much deeper than rain forest topsoil (right).

topsoil

topsoil

To Keep Earth Just Right

A spacecraft lands on Earth's neighbor, Venus, and starts taking pictures of the bleak, rocky surface. In less than two hours, all signals from the landed craft stop. The 900°F heat and crushing pressure are too much even for a robot explorer. They would be deadly to anything living on Earth.

Millions of miles away on another neighbor, Mars, a sudden storm lifts red dust high into the sky. Spacecraft, too, visit the red planet without finding a sign of life. The air on Mars is too thin to breathe and at night the temperatures can drop to −150°F. That's colder than any place on Earth and too cold for anything living on Earth.

Earth remains the only planet where life is known to exist. It is not too hot nor too cold for plants, insects, fishes, birds, people—every living thing. Keeping the temperatures on Earth just right for life is one of nature's great accomplishments.

heat escaping

atmosphere

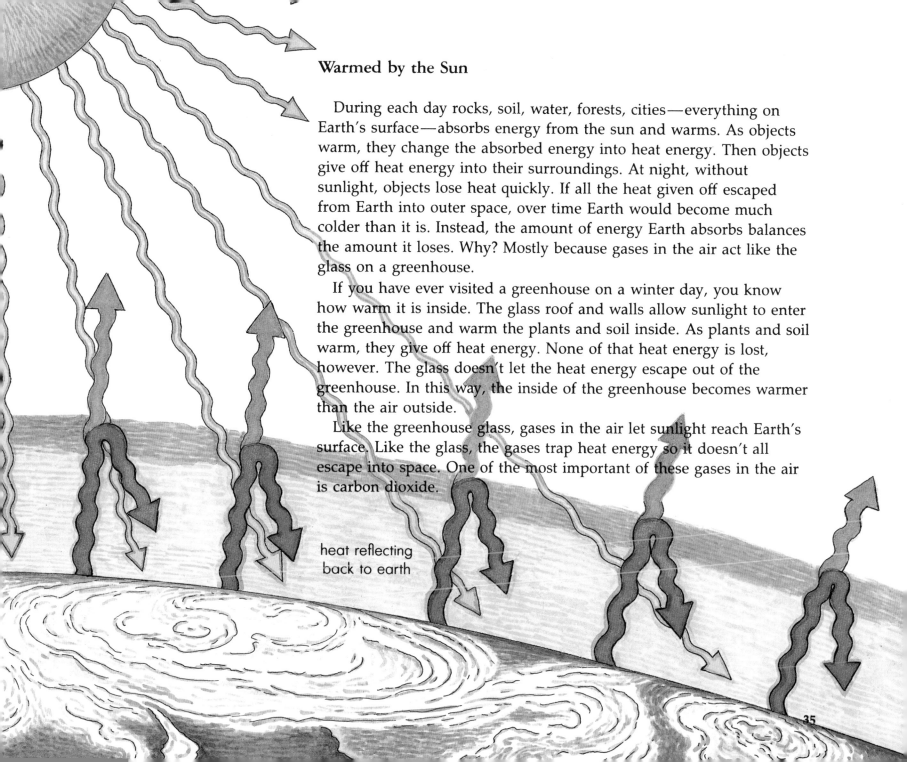

Warmed by the Sun

During each day rocks, soil, water, forests, cities—everything on Earth's surface—absorbs energy from the sun and warms. As objects warm, they change the absorbed energy into heat energy. Then objects give off heat energy into their surroundings. At night, without sunlight, objects lose heat quickly. If all the heat given off escaped from Earth into outer space, over time Earth would become much colder than it is. Instead, the amount of energy Earth absorbs balances the amount it loses. Why? Mostly because gases in the air act like the glass on a greenhouse.

If you have ever visited a greenhouse on a winter day, you know how warm it is inside. The glass roof and walls allow sunlight to enter the greenhouse and warm the plants and soil inside. As plants and soil warm, they give off heat energy. None of that heat energy is lost, however. The glass doesn't let the heat energy escape out of the greenhouse. In this way, the inside of the greenhouse becomes warmer than the air outside.

Like the greenhouse glass, gases in the air let sunlight reach Earth's surface. Like the glass, the gases trap heat energy so it doesn't all escape into space. One of the most important of these gases in the air is carbon dioxide.

heat reflecting
back to earth

35

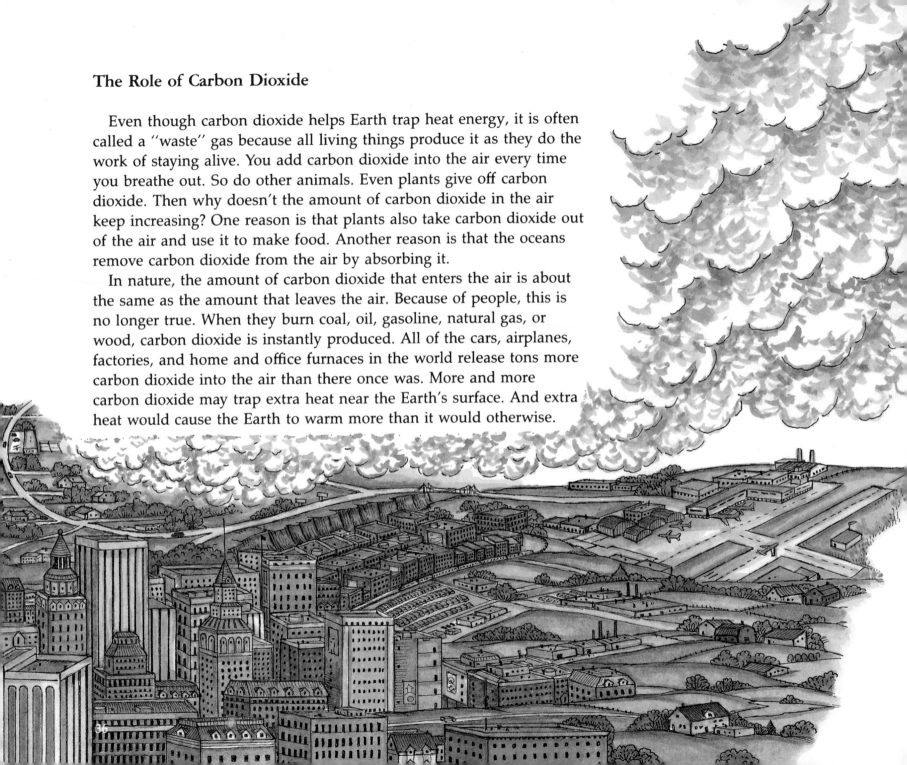

The Role of Carbon Dioxide

Even though carbon dioxide helps Earth trap heat energy, it is often called a "waste" gas because all living things produce it as they do the work of staying alive. You add carbon dioxide into the air every time you breathe out. So do other animals. Even plants give off carbon dioxide. Then why doesn't the amount of carbon dioxide in the air keep increasing? One reason is that plants also take carbon dioxide out of the air and use it to make food. Another reason is that the oceans remove carbon dioxide from the air by absorbing it.

In nature, the amount of carbon dioxide that enters the air is about the same as the amount that leaves the air. Because of people, this is no longer true. When they burn coal, oil, gasoline, natural gas, or wood, carbon dioxide is instantly produced. All of the cars, airplanes, factories, and home and office furnaces in the world release tons more carbon dioxide into the air than there once was. More and more carbon dioxide may trap extra heat near the Earth's surface. And extra heat would cause the Earth to warm more than it would otherwise.

If Earth starts to warm up, the overall weather, or climate, in many places could change. Crops won't be able to grow where they do now. There will be more violent storms, and more parts of the world will turn into deserts. Even the ice at the North and South Poles may melt, adding so much water into the oceans that sea levels will rise flooding coastal cities and towns.

Scientists need to learn a lot more about how climate works before they will know for sure what will happen if Earth warms. Until they do, one way to keep down the amount of carbon dioxide in the air is to save the rain forests. Think of the huge number of saved plants that would keep removing carbon dioxide to make more food. Now think of how much extra carbon dioxide would be added to the air if each and every rain forest plant were burned! The fewer plants, the less carbon dioxide is absorbed. The rain forests are an important part of nature's way of getting the job done and keeping Earth just right.

carbon dioxide absorbed by rain forests

Nature Needs the Rain Forests

Once there were dinosaurs. Now there are none. Once there were no insects or birds or flowers. Now they are everywhere. Once all the continents were joined together into one giant land. Today the continents spread around the globe. The Earth has changed over hundreds of millions of years. The species living on Earth have also changed.

How living things change over a very long time allows new species to develop, or evolve from the old. Insects, birds, flowering plants, and mammals all evolved from living things that came before them.

Step into the rain forests and from the water-filled bromeliads to the pitcher plants, from the tent bats to the magnificent quetzals, from the gold beetles to the red frogs, you will see how each species fits into the world around it so that each species can survive.

Since life on Earth first began, there have been periods when many, many kinds of living things died out, or became extinct. The most famous took place about 65 million years ago when the dinosaurs died out forever. Were the dinosaurs and tens of thousands of other species killed off because the world's climate changed? Were they struck down by a terrible disease? Did an asteroid striking Earth or tremendous volcanic eruptions put an end to the giant reptiles? No one knows for sure.

Scientists are trying to learn what causes large numbers of species to become extinct. The one thing scientists do know is that every time there has been a great extinction all living things did not die. For example, whatever caused the dinosaurs to disappear did not kill many kinds of small mammals that lived around the same time.

38

Allosaurus

Deinotherium

dodo

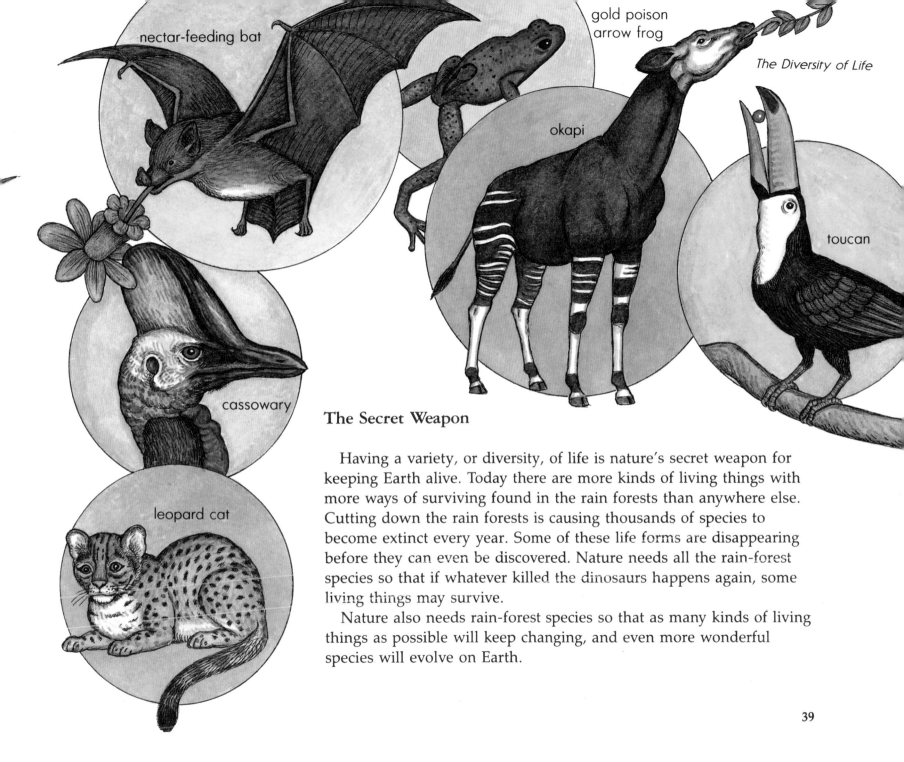

nectar-feeding bat

gold poison
arrow frog

okapi

toucan

cassowary

leopard cat

The Secret Weapon

Having a variety, or diversity, of life is nature's secret weapon for keeping Earth alive. Today there are more kinds of living things with more ways of surviving found in the rain forests than anywhere else. Cutting down the rain forests is causing thousands of species to become extinct every year. Some of these life forms are disappearing before they can even be discovered. Nature needs all the rain-forest species so that if whatever killed the dinosaurs happens again, some living things may survive.

Nature also needs rain-forest species so that as many kinds of living things as possible will keep changing, and even more wonderful species will evolve on Earth.

6 SAVING THE RAIN FORESTS

As long as there are rain forests, people will keep finding plants and animals they can use.

There are so many reasons to save the tropical rain forests. For all the plants, animals, and people, these forests are the perfect places to live. For the soil they are protection from the hot sun and drenching rains. Cities and towns hundreds of miles away depend on them to prevent floods. Doctors need the rain forests for medicines, grocers for foods, florists for house plants. In one way or another the rain forests touch just about everyone's life. They are a vital part of how nature keeps Earth alive.

What about the people in the tropics trying to build a better life? They do have the right to use their land to help themselves and their countries. However, destroying the rain forests is the wrong way to go about it. The best future they can ensure for their children and their grandchildren will come from keeping the rain forests full of life.

Tropical rain forests are rich in renewable resources such as fruits, berries, nuts, flowers, and latex. Instead of losing everything the rain forests have to offer and ruining the soil, people in the tropics can keep earning their living by tapping the forests' renewable riches. And as mysteries such as how the miracle fruit's protein can be so sweet are solved, who knows how many more new products will come from the rain forests?

Because the alarm has been sounded by nature lovers and scientists, many tropical nations are starting to reclaim their rain forests. But they need help from everyone who cares about this planet to bring the destruction to a halt.

giant Amazonian river turtle

rosy periwinkle

amaranth

cocoa

coconut

capsicum pepper

cinnamon

allspice

cloves

vanilla bean

Brazil nut

nutmeg

rattan

41

What You Can Do

It doesn't matter if the rain forests are nearby or thousands of miles away from where you live. There are steps that you can take to save the rain forests.

First, you can write to elected government leaders and ask them to set aside money that will help tropical nations protect their rain forests. You can find the addresses at your local library.

Secondly, you can write or call any or all of the groups listed on page 43 for information about how they are trying to save the rain forests. If you show this information to your parents, teacher, or scout leader, they may come up with ways you and your friends can raise money to donate to one or more of these groups. Some students are already raising money to buy pieces of rain forests. When enough pieces are purchased, they will be joined together so no one can harm them.

You can also ask adults not to buy anything made of teak, mahogany, or ebony. These woods come from rain-forest trees that are in danger. When the demand drops, fewer and fewer trees will be cut down. At the same time, you can point out tropical fruits, nuts, oils, teas, spices, honey, and rattan for sale. The greater the demand for these renewable products, the more tropical workers can make their living from them without having to destroy the rain forests.

So tell your family. Tell your friends. Tell your teachers. Working together, people can save the tropical rain forests.

Children's Rainforest
P.O. Box 936
Lewiston, Maine 04240

Conservation International
1015 18th Street NW
Suite 1000
Washington, D.C. 20036
202/429-5660

National Audubon Society
666 Pennsylvania Avenue SE
Washington, D.C. 20003
202/547-9009

National Wildlife Federation
1400 16th Street NW
Washington, D.C. 20036
202/797-6800

World Wildlife Fund
1250 24th Street NW
Washington, D.C. 20037
202/293-4800

The Nature Conservancy
1815 North Lynn Street
Arlington, Virginia 22209
703/841-5300

Rainforest Action Network
450 Sansome, Suite 700
San Francisco, California 94111
415/398-4404

Smithsonian Tropical Research
Institute
Unit 0948
APO AA 34002-0948

Sierra Club
730 Polk Street
San Francisco, California 94109
415/776-2211

Tree Amigos/Center for
Environmental Study
143 Bostwick NE
Grand Rapids, MI 49503
616/771-3935

RAIN FORESTS AROUND THE WORLD

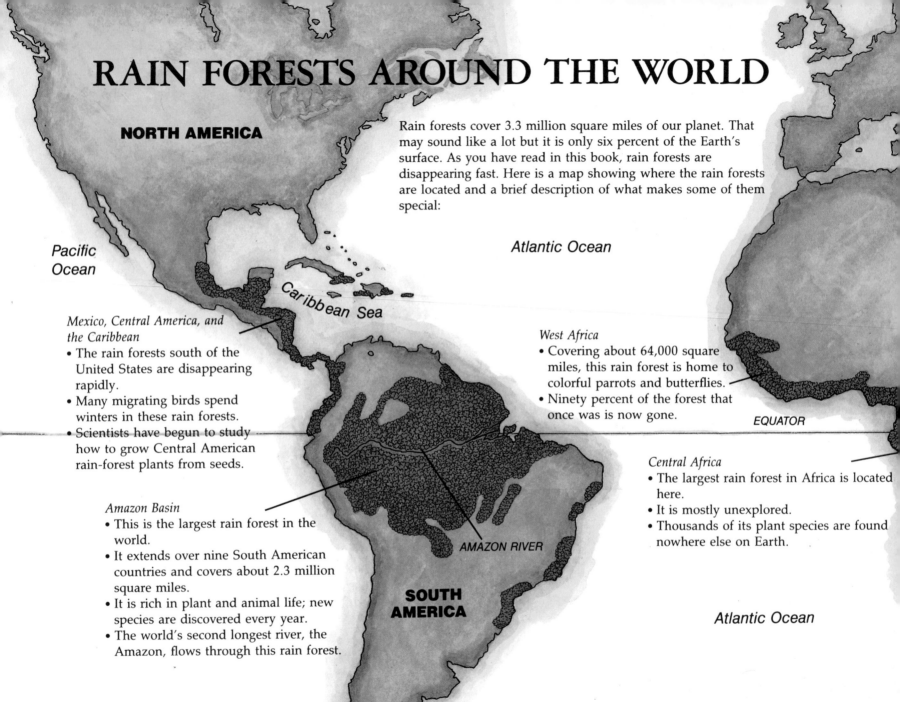

NORTH AMERICA

Rain forests cover 3.3 million square miles of our planet. That may sound like a lot but it is only six percent of the Earth's surface. As you have read in this book, rain forests are disappearing fast. Here is a map showing where the rain forests are located and a brief description of what makes some of them special:

Pacific Ocean

Atlantic Ocean

Caribbean Sea

Mexico, Central America, and the Caribbean
- The rain forests south of the United States are disappearing rapidly.
- Many migrating birds spend winters in these rain forests.
- Scientists have begun to study how to grow Central American rain-forest plants from seeds.

West Africa
- Covering about 64,000 square miles, this rain forest is home to colorful parrots and butterflies.
- Ninety percent of the forest that once was is now gone.

EQUATOR

Amazon Basin
- This is the largest rain forest in the world.
- It extends over nine South American countries and covers about 2.3 million square miles.
- It is rich in plant and animal life; new species are discovered every year.
- The world's second longest river, the Amazon, flows through this rain forest.

AMAZON RIVER

Central Africa
- The largest rain forest in Africa is located here.
- It is mostly unexplored.
- Thousands of its plant species are found nowhere else on Earth.

SOUTH AMERICA

Atlantic Ocean

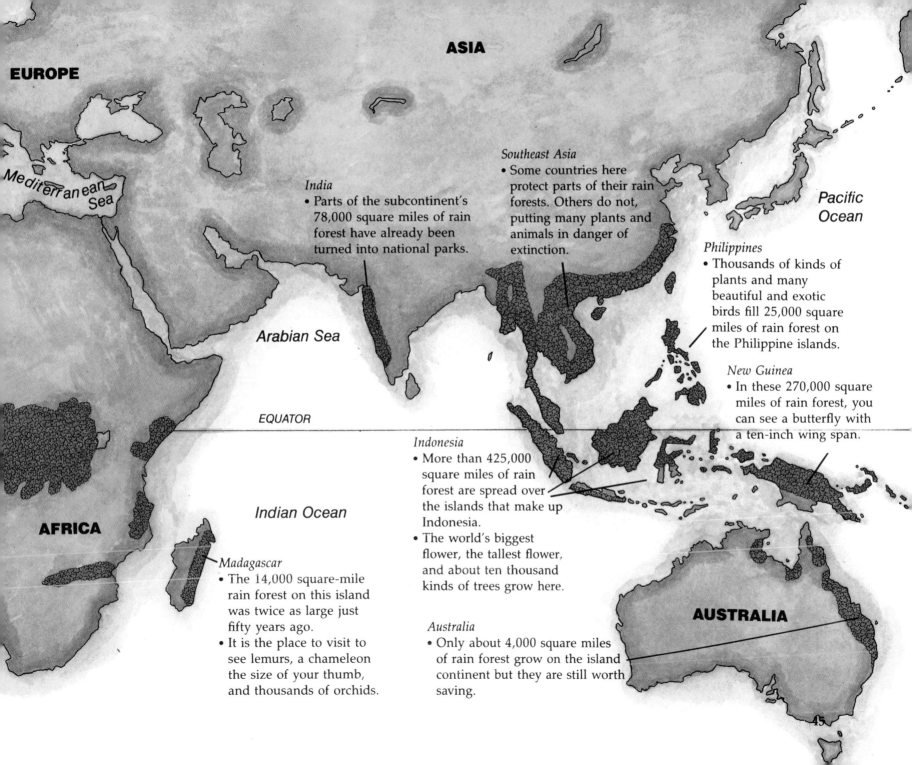

EUROPE

ASIA

Mediterranean Sea

AFRICA

Arabian Sea

India
• Parts of the subcontinent's 78,000 square miles of rain forest have already been turned into national parks.

Southeast Asia
• Some countries here protect parts of their rain forests. Others do not, putting many plants and animals in danger of extinction.

Pacific Ocean

Philippines
• Thousands of kinds of plants and many beautiful and exotic birds fill 25,000 square miles of rain forest on the Philippine islands.

New Guinea
• In these 270,000 square miles of rain forest, you can see a butterfly with a ten-inch wing span.

EQUATOR

Indian Ocean

Indonesia
• More than 425,000 square miles of rain forest are spread over the islands that make up Indonesia.
• The world's biggest flower, the tallest flower, and about ten thousand kinds of trees grow here.

Madagascar
• The 14,000 square-mile rain forest on this island was twice as large just fifty years ago.
• It is the place to visit to see lemurs, a chameleon the size of your thumb, and thousands of orchids.

Australia
• Only about 4,000 square miles of rain forest grow on the island continent but they are still worth saving.

AUSTRALIA

45

FURTHER READING

Aldis, Rodney. *Rainforests.* New York: Dillon, 1991.

Azimov, Isaac. *Why Are the Rain Forests Vanishing?* Milwaukee, WI: Gareth Stevens, Inc., 1992.

Bramwell, Martyn. *The Environment and Conservation.* Englewood Cliffs, NJ: Prentice-Hall, 1992.

Baker, Lucy. *Life in the Rainforests.* New York: Franklin Watts, 1990.

Catchpole, Clive. *The Living World—Jungles.* New York: Dial Books, 1985.

Cherry, Lynne. *The Great Kapok Tree: A Tale of the Amazon Rain Forest.* New York: Gulliver Books, 1990.

Chinery, Michael. *Rainforest Animals.* New York: Random House, 1992.

Crump, Donald J. *The Emerald Realm: Earth's Precious Rain Forests.* Washington, D.C.: National Geographic Society, 1990.

Dorros, Arthur. *Rain Forest Secrets.* New York: Scholastic, 1990.

Earth Works Group. *50 Simple Things Kids Can Do To Save the Earth.* Kansas City, KS: Andrews and McMeel, 1990.

Forsyth, Adrian. *Journey Through a Tropical Jungle.* New York: Simon & Schuster, 1989.

George, Jean Craighead. *One Day in the Tropical Rain Forest.* New York: Crowell, 1990.

Goodman, Billy. *The Rain Forest.* New York: Little Brown, 1992.

Greenhaven Press editors. *How Can Rain Forests Be Saved?* San Diego, CA: Greenhaven Press, 1991.

Hare, Tony. *Rainforest Destruction.* New York: Franklin Watts, 1990.

Holmes, Anita. *I Can Save the Earth: A Kid's Handbook for Keeping Earth Healthy and Green.* New York: Julian Messner, 1993.

Johnston, Damian. *Make Your Own Rain Forest.* New York: Lodestar Books, 1993.

Kricher, John C. and Gordon Morrison. *A Field Guide to Tropical Forests Coloring Book.* Boston: Houghton Mifflin, 1991.

Landau, Elaine. *Tropical Rain Forests Around the World.* New York: Franklin Watts, 1990.

Lewis, Scott. *The Rain Forest Book.* New York: Berkley Books, 1993.

Miller, Christina G. and Louise A. Berry. *A Jungle Rescue: Saving the New World Tropical Rainforests.* New York: Atheneum, 1991.

National Wildlife Federation editors. *Rain Forests: Tropical Treasures.* Vienna, VA: National Wildlife Federation, 1991.

Perry, Donald. *Life Above the Jungle Floor.* New York: Simon & Schuster, 1986.

Pope, Joyce. *Plants of the Tropics.* New York: Facts-on-File, 1990.

Prosser, Robert. *Disappearing Rainforest.* London: Batsford, 1988.

Ross, Suzanne. *What's in the Rainforest?: One Hundred and Six Answers from A to Z.* Los Angeles, CA: Enchanted Rainforest Press, 1991.

Sierra Club. *Sierra Club Rain Forest Theater: A Pop-up-and-Play Activity Book.* San Francisco, CA: Sierra Club Books for Children, 1992.

Siy, Alexandra. *The Brazilian Rainforest.* New York: Dillon, 1992.

Taylor, Barbara. *Rain Forest.* New York: Dorling Kindersley, 1992.

 # INDEX

About the Author

Donald Silver writes about science and nature for children of all ages. He is the author of *The Animal World* and *Earth: The Ever-Changing Planet*. His series of books, *One Small Square*, take a close-up look at plants and animals where they live. Mr. Silver also writes educational materials. He lives in New York City.

About the Illustrator

Patricia J. Wynne has illustrated over fifty books for children. Most, like *The Human Body and How It Works* and the *One Small Square* series, focus on living things, large and small. In addition, she has illustrated *Look What We've Brought You From Mexico* and numerous activity books. Ms. Wynne's scientific illustrations have appeared in the *New York Times*, *Scientific American*, *Natural History*, and *Smithsonian*. She lives in New York City and has collaborated with Donald Silver for more than ten years.